£12.95

ALL
THAT BASS
...PLUS 11 MORE TOP HITS

Published by
Wise Publications
14-15 Berners Street, London W1T 3LJ, UK.

Exclusive Distributors:

Music Sales Limited
Distribution Centre, Newmarket Road,
Bury St Edmunds, Suffolk IP33 3YB, UK.

Music Sales Pty Limited
4th floor, Lisgar House, 30-32 Carrington Street,
Sydney, NSW 2000, Australia.

Order No. AM1010636
ISBN: 978-1-78305-980-5
This book © Copyright 2015 Wise Publications,
a division of Music Sales Limited.

Unauthorised reproduction of any part of this
publication by any means including photocopying
is an infringement of copyright.

Edited by Jenni Norey.
Cover design by Tim Field.

Printed in the EU.

PIANO • VOCAL • GUITAR

ALL ABOUT THAT BASS
...PLUS 11 MORE TOP HITS

WISE PUBLICATIONS
part of The Music Sales Group
London / New York / Paris / Sydney / Copenhagen / Berlin / Madrid / Hong Kong / Tokyo

Your Guarantee of Quality:

As publishers, we strive to produce every book
to the highest commercial standards.

This book has been carefully designed to minimise awkward page turns
and to make playing from it a real pleasure.

Particular care has been given to specifying acid-free, neutral-sized paper
made from pulps which have not been elemental chlorine bleached.
This pulp is from farmed sustainable forests and was produced
with special regard for the environment.

Throughout, the printing and binding have been planned to ensure a sturdy,
attractive publication which should give years of enjoyment.

If your copy fails to meet our high standards, please inform us
and we will gladly replace it.

www.musicsales.com

ALL ABOUT THAT BASS • MEGHAN TRAINOR • 6

BLAME IT ON ME • GEORGE EZRA • 12

HOLD BACK THE RIVER • JAMES BAY • 18

LIKE I CAN • SAM SMITH • 25

NIGHT CHANGES • ONE DIRECTION • 34

REAL LOVE • TOM ODELL • 30

THESE DAYS • TAKE THAT • 46

THINKING OUT LOUD • ED SHEERAN • 41

UPTOWN FUNK! • MARK RONSON FEAT. BRUNO MARS • 54

WILDEST DREAMS • TAYLOR SWIFT • 62

WRAPPED UP • OLLY MURS • 68

YOURS • ELLA HENDERSON • 76

All About That Bass

Words & Music by Kevin Kadish & Meghan Trainor

Blame It On Me

Words & Music by Joel Pott & George Ezra Barnett

Hold Back The River

Words & Music by Iain Archer & James Bay

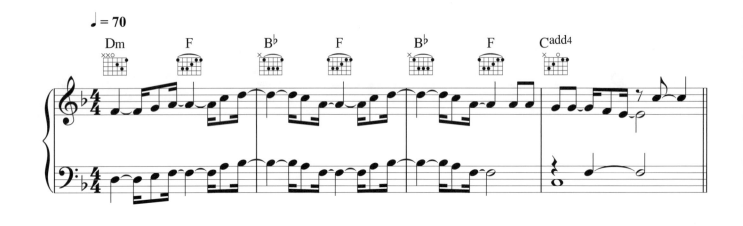

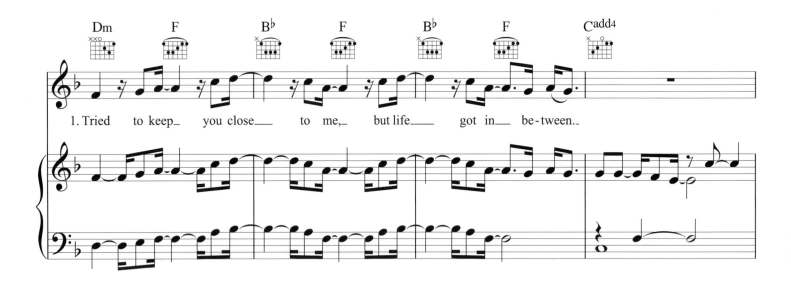

1. Tried to keep you close to me, but life got in be-tween.

Tried to square not be-ing there, but think that I should have been. Hold

© Copyright 2014 Kobalt Music Services Limited/B Unique Music.
Kobalt Music Publishing Limited.
All Rights Reserved. International Copyright Secured.

Like I Can

Words & Music by Sam Smith & Matthew Prime

Real Love

Words & Music by John Lennon

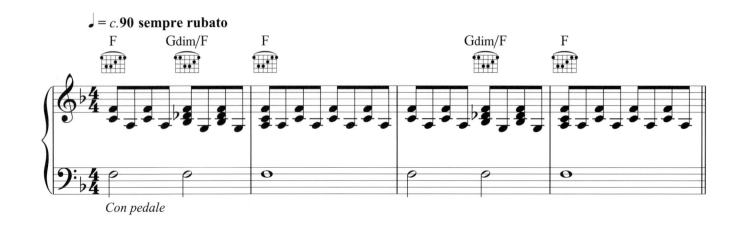
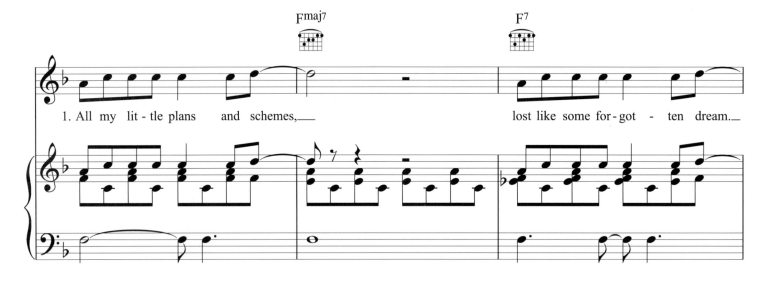
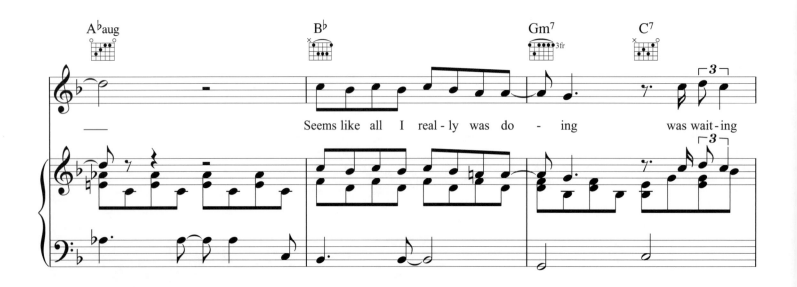

© Copyright 1988 & 1995 Lenono Music.
All Rights Reserved. International Copyright Secured.

Night Changes

Words & Music by John Ryan, Jamie Scott, Julian Bunetta, Harry Styles,
Niall Horan, Liam Payne, Zain Malik & Louis Tomlinson

© Copyright 2014 BMG Platinum Songs US/Holy Cannoli Music/Music Of Big Deal/Bob Erotik Music/The Family Songbook.
Universal/MCA Music Limited/EMI Music Publishing/BMG Rights Management (US) LLC, a BMG Chrysalis company/PPM Music Ltd.
All Rights Reserved. International Copyright Secured.

Thinking Out Loud

Words & Music by Ed Sheeran & Amy Wadge

Uptown Funk!

Words & Music by Mark Ronson, Philip Lawrence, Jeffrey Bhasker,
Peter Hernandez, Nicholaus Williams & Devon Gallaspy

© Copyright 2014 Copyright Control.
All Rights Reserved. International Copyright Secured.

Wildest Dreams

Words & Music by Taylor Swift, Shellback
& Max Martin

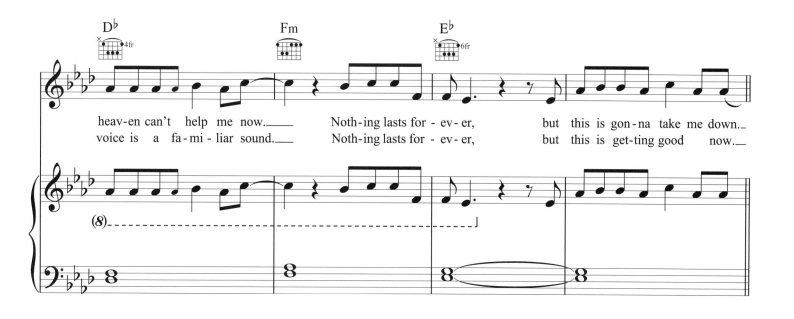

Wrapped Up

Words & Music by Stephen Robson, Claude Kelly,
Olly Murs & Travis McCoy

© Copyright 2014 EMI April Music Incorporated/Salli Isaak Music Publishing Limited/Imagem CV/Temps D'Avance.
Universal Music Publishing Limited/Copyright Control/EMI Music Publishing Limited/Imagem Music.
All Rights Reserved. International Copyright Secured.

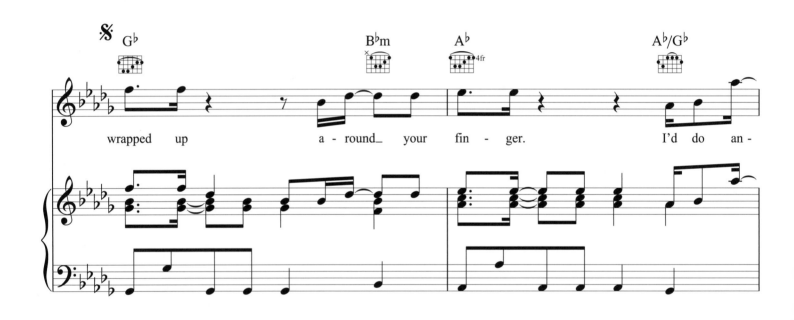
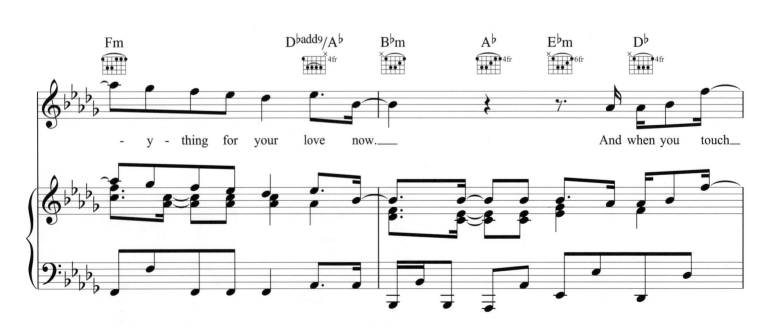

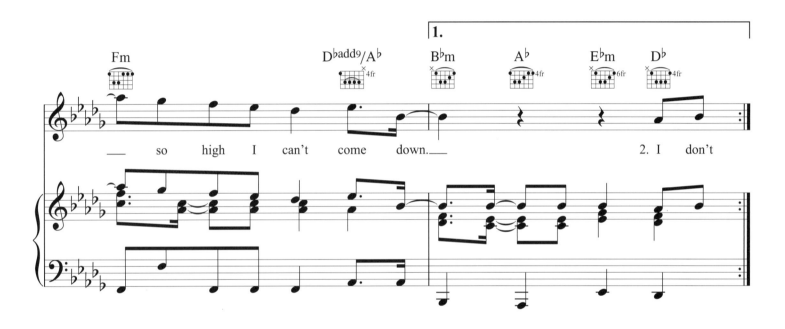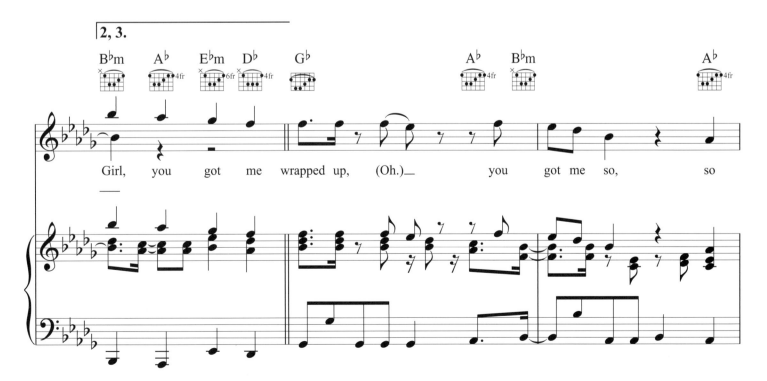

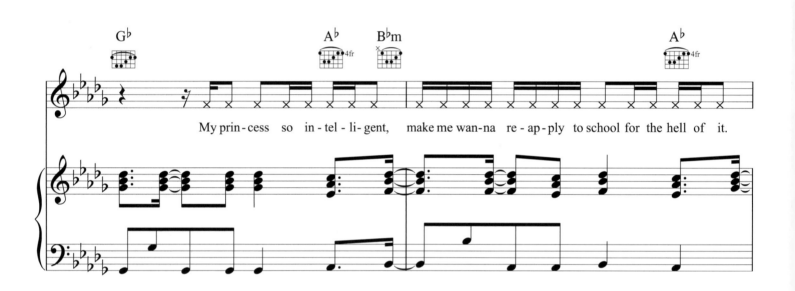
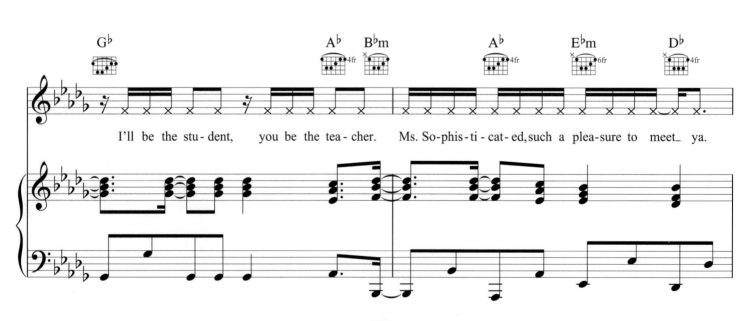

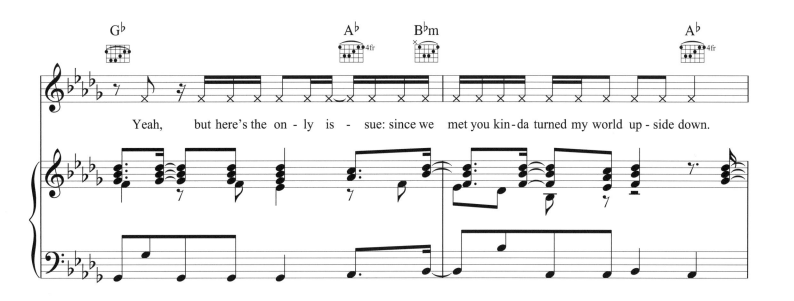
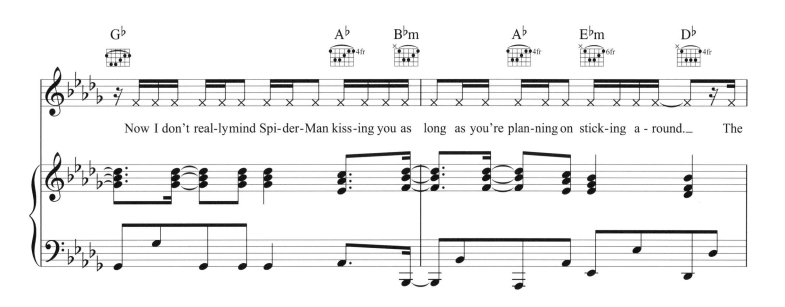
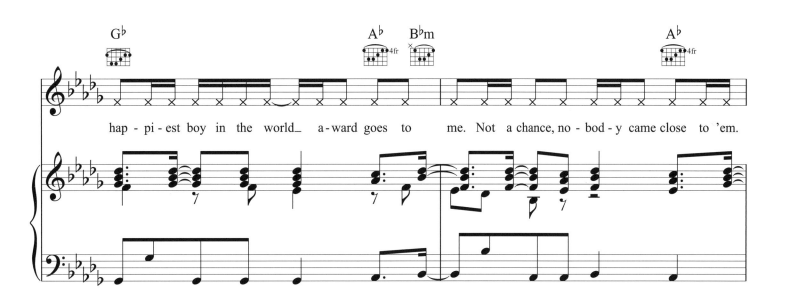

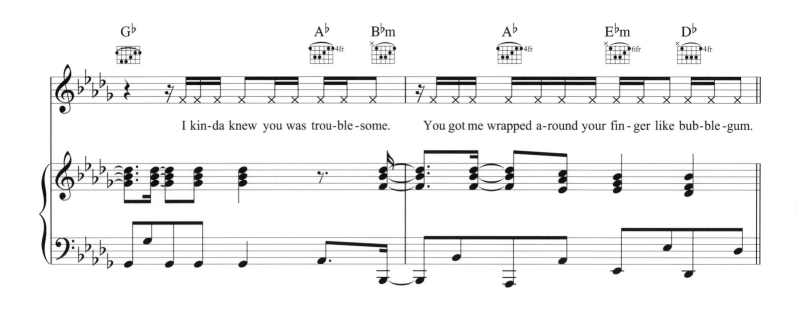
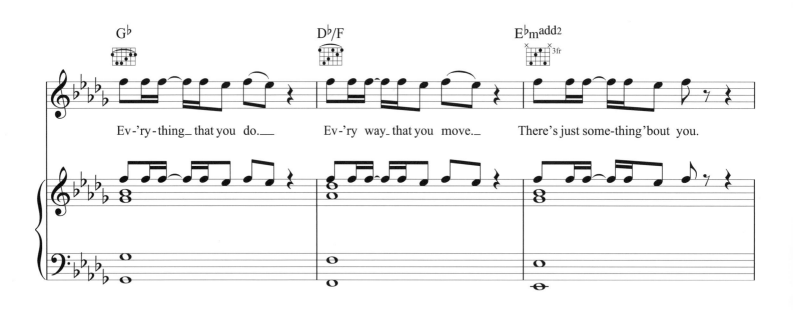
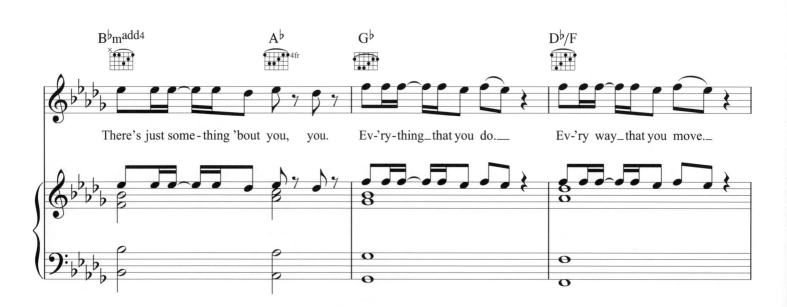

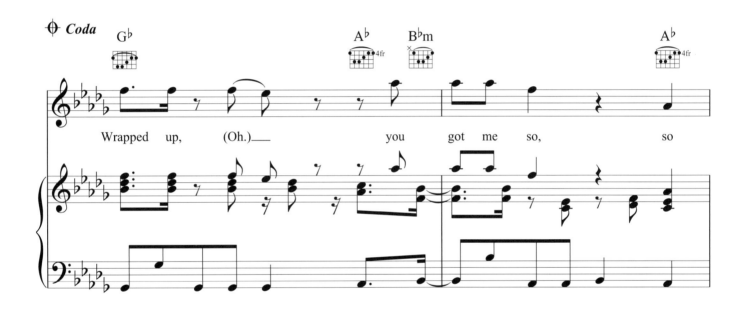

Yours

Words & Music by Joshua Record & Ella Henderson

Bringing you the words and the music

All the latest music in print... rock & pop plus jazz, blues, country, classical and the best in West End show scores.

- Books to match your favourite CDs.

- Book-and-CD titles with high quality backing tracks for you to play along to. Now you can play guitar or piano with your favourite artist... or simply sing along!

- Audition songbooks with CD backing tracks for both male and female singers for all those with stars in their eyes.

- Can't read music? No problem, you can still play all the hits with our wide range of chord songbooks.

- Check out our range of instrumental tutorial titles, taking you from novice to expert in no time at all!

- Musical show scores include *The Phantom Of The Opera*, *Les Misérables*, *Mamma Mia* and many more hit productions.

- DVD master classes featuring the techniques of top artists.

Visit your local music shop or, in case of difficulty, contact the Marketing Department, Music Sales Limited, Newmarket Road, Bury St Edmunds, Suffolk, IP33 3YB, UK
marketing@musicsales.co.uk